Affectionate Writings:

A God Inspired Devotional to Help You Through the Stresses of this World.

Cheyenne Moody

Affectionate Writings

ISBN: 9781078749695

DEDICATION

It is with much gratefulness that I dedicate this book, first and foremost, to God. My Abba, my Father, the one true God. If I did not have God in my life as my rock and salvation, I would not be where I am today. Keeping Jesus the center of my entire life, has been the most rewarding thing that I could ever do. He has never left me, nor has He forsaken me. Upon writing this book, I prayed that He would give me the words to write, and He has done just that. Thank you, Father, for guiding me, protecting me, and loving me all the days of my life.

I also dedicate this book to my friend, Kari Whatley. She has played such a fantastic role in my life and has helped me grow in so many ways. Upon finishing each devotional, she read them, and her kind encouraging words are what helped me have a passion for continuing my writings. There were some poems that I felt were subpar, yet those were the ones she complimented me on the most, without even knowing that those were a struggle for me. I am so blessed that God allowed our paths to cross and that I can call her and her husband, Jason, not only friends but also family. Thank you for the compassion you have shown me thus far.

Last, but certainly not least, I would like to dedicate this book to the person who inspired me to write it in the first place. I want to dedicate this book to the man who inspired the title, genre, and existence of this book. I dedicate this devotional to Mr. Johnny Foote. He was one of the most God-fearing, God-loving men that I knew. He touched more lives on this earth than most can even dream of touching. I always thought of him as a grandfather figure to me. He was a true prophet of God, and I am so blessed to had known him in the way that I did. I will forever cherish the moments that I had with him and will forever cherish the prophetic words I received from him. He was indeed one of a kind. The heavens are so lucky to have him now, helping to prepare for the day that heaven fights the final fight and wins the grand prize.

CONTENTS

Affectionate Writings

Cheyenne Moody

ACKNOWLEDGMENTS

I count one of my biggest blessings in life as being raised in a single-parent household with a dad whose top priority was to make sure his children grew up in the way of the Lord. I accredit my love for Jesus and my eagerness to learn more about Christ to my dad. He has shown me what a father's love is, and he has helped me learn that if I want something in life, I must work hard for it. I also accredit so much of my accomplishments to my brother. Every little girl wants to grow up to be just like their big brother, or at least I did. Seeing him use the gifts that God has given him for ministry and good is genuinely inspiring. It has helped me take my talents and put them to use in a Christlike way. I strive to help others reach Christ and their full potential using the gifts given to me because I grew up watching my dad and brother do the same. My life has not been perfect, nor by any means has it been easy. I have been through my fair share of ups and downs, I have experienced hurt, heartache, stress, worry. However, I have also experienced love, joy, blessings, accomplishments, and so much more. I have learned that the secret to a happy life, the secret to so much, is so simple. The secret to a happy life is prayer. Yep, that is it, prayer. I have written this book in hopes that it will help you or someone you know get through the hardships that this world throws at you. The topics in this book are all things I have experienced at some point in my life. However, I have overcome these situations and circumstances through prayer and support from loved ones. I know you can get through your hardships too. Just keep praying, keep the faith, and make God the center of your entire existence!

Preface

What do you see when you look in the mirror? I hope you see a powerful, beautiful, or handsome, capable human being. You might not be the best at sports, math, social skills, etc. however, God has designed each person on earth with different strengths and weaknesses (or areas for improvement.) My hope with writing this book is to encourage those all around the world, and to let them know that life is not perfect. It will have roadblocks and bumps along the way, but if you keep your head up, your eyes forward, and a positive mindset, then you will be okay. You are destined for great things! God created you in His image and likeness, it says so in Genesis 1:27. His plans for you far exceed anything you have in mind for yourself! You are a rare gem in His eyes; never forget that! If you ever feel alone, remember that God will never leave you nor forsake you! Do the things you think you cannot do! Do the things you are told you are not good enough or strong enough to do, because let me tell you: God says you are good enough! He says you are strong enough. He says you are beautiful or handsome enough! All you must do is seek His help and guidance, and my friend, you will be unstoppable. You will be a force to be reckoned with! Be a light unto others and an example to the nations. Do not worry about living up to the world's standards; be the best YOU that you can be!

With much love,

Cheyenne

1

Love

YOURSELF, not

who others

want you to be.

Uniqueness

"I praise You, for I am fearfully and wonderfully made. Wonderful are Your works; my soul knows it well."

Psalm 139:14

God created you to shine

He placed every hair on your head

Every freckle on your body

Every finger every toe

God created you to shine

He knit you together so perfectly

He gave you all your weird quirks

Every crazy habit

Every single feature you possess

God made you to shine

If God made us to shine, if He intended for us to be unique, why would we want to change that? Why would we want to be like someone else, have someone else's hair, smile, life? The world sets such high standards, but that doesn't mean we have to abide by those standards. So what if every hair on your head isn't entirely in place, or your clothes aren't as high end as others. So what if you don't drive the newest car or have the neatest house. God didn't create you to follow the standards this world has set. He made you to be you to spread His love and His word. God didn't create you in hopes that you would turn out to be just like Sam or Sally. No, God created you to stand out. God created you because He loves you for you if everyone was the same, what a boring world it would be.

Reflection:

What makes you unique?

___

___

___

How are you going to live more unique and not so much according to worldly standards?

___

___

___

Challenge:

I challenge you to live uniquely. Sure, you can like some of the same things as someone else, but make sure you take time out of your day to ask yourself if you are living the life that God wants you to live, or if you are living life according to the world's standards.

Words of Affirmation:

I am loved for who I am

I am good enough just as myself

I am God's creation

I AM UNIQUE

2

Any progress is good progress!

Never Give Up on your Dreams

"I can do all things through Christ who strengthens me."

Philippians 4:13

Keep going. You are almost there

I know the road may seem long and your dreams may seem unreachable

I know there may have been setbacks and obstacles to overcome

But keep going, you are almost there.

I know others might be passing you up and that can feel discouraging

I know you may be tired and frustrated

But keep going, you are almost there.

In life, we set goals for ourselves, some short term, others long term — some right within reach, and others so far away. Sometimes we are on the brink of just giving up and walking away, but keep pressing on. When you feel like quitting, like it's never going to happen, remember why you set the goal in the first place. Remember that God is with you and will catch you when you fall. Remember that even though you may have fallen a few times, God will be there with His hand stretched out, ready to help you get back on your feet. See, what often happens is we only tend to look at the end game, the big picture. Sometimes that can get overwhelming, and you may feel like you are never going to get there. Instead, why don't we try to focus on the steps we need to take to get there. Take it one day at a time, step by step. Look where you began and where you are now and ask yourself, "have I made any progress at all?" because any good progress is better than no progress. Every step in the right direction will get you closer to your goal. So, hold onto hope. Believe in yourself and ask God for His help and guidance through it all.

Reflection:

What are some goals you have, or want to have, set for yourself?

____

____

____

How are you going to respond when you come across obstacles and/or setbacks, because you will have a few of each?

____

____

____

Challenge:

I challenge you to dream big. When things don’t go quite as planned, I challenge you to keep your head held high and keep pressing on. I challenge you to sit down with your goals in mind and come up with the steps needed to reach said goal. Lastly, I challenge you to take your goals and dreams step by step, one day at a time, all while making sure you are keeping God first.

Words of Affirmation:

I can do this

I will reach my goals

Whatever comes my way, I will stand tall and stay encouraged

With God, all things are possible

3

You were Created with Purpose!

My Life has Purpose

"For I know the plans I have for you declares the Lord, plans to prosper you and not to harm you, plans to give you hope and a future."

Jeremiah 29:11

Your life has a great purpose

You may not see it now,

You may not feel like you are doing anything special, but

Your life has a great purpose

In time, God will reveal His plans

In time, you will find your calling in this world

Your life has a great purpose

We look at the world around us and see surgeons saving lives, firefighters putting out fires, pastors leading the congregation. We hear about these people and see what great things they are doing, how they have found their calling, and how it is changing bits and pieces of the world. Then we look at ourselves and think, man, why have I not found my calling yet? But what if you have? You might not be world renown, but who cares? If you have a strong passion and are doing what makes you happy, if you are going in the way God is directing you, then that is good enough! You do not have to have a three-figure job or a fancy career to matter. Just be who God created you to be, only travel the road God has paved for you, and you will fulfill your purpose.

Reflection:

Do you feel like you have found your purpose in life? If so, what is it?

____

____

____

If you are still searching for your purpose, how will you stay encouraged while you wait for it to be revealed?

____

____

____

____

Challenge:

I challenge you to stop comparing yourself to others. I challenge you to look at your life and point out all the great things you have done thus far. I challenge you to remember that God created you because He needs you. He will reveal His plan soon enough.

Words of Affirmation:

My life has a great purpose

I will do great things

God has big plans for me

4

I am Prepared because I Wear the Full Armor of God!

Be Prepared

"Therefore, put on the full armor of God, so that when the day of evil comes, you may be able to stand your ground..."

Ephesians 6:13

In the morning when you wake

Put on the armor of God

Before you lay your head down at night to sleep,

Put on the armor of God

When everything seems hopeless

When it feels like the whole world is against you,

Put on the armor of God

Have you ever been in a situation where you are doing all of the right things, and you feel like you are on the path God has set for you, but for some unknown reason things get super hard all of a sudden; almost like everything is trying to steer you off course? The bible tells us to take up the full armor of God so that we can stand our ground against the enemy. The enemy is always at work, especially when we grow closer and closer to God and towards what God has planned for us. It is so essential to make sure that you are prepared and protected in those moments when the devil tries to discourage you or lead you astray. Take up God's authoritative, protective armor every single day, and in those moments of hardship or trouble, declare the armor again and again.

Reflection:

Have you experienced a time of sudden turmoil that came out of nowhere? How did you overcome it?

____

____

____

List the full armor of God on the lines below.

____

____

____

Challenge:

I challenge you to wake up every morning and put on the full armor of God. I challenge you that in your times of turmoil or chaos, remember the armor you put on and declare that the devil cannot overcome the power armor you wear.

Words of Affirmation:

God's armor makes me strong

God's armor puts a hedge of protection around me

God's armor can defeat all strongholds

5

Sometimes, the most courageous thing you can do is ask for help!

Asking for Help is Courageous

"Ask, and it will be given to you; seek, and you will find; knock, and it will be opened to you."

Matthew 7:7

Don't be afraid to ask for help; everyone needs it

You don't have to do it all alone

You don't have to pretend like you have it all under control

Don't be afraid to ask for help; everyone needs it

Asking for help makes you strong

Asking for help makes you humble

Don't be scared to ask for help; everyone needs it

So many people are afraid to ask for help. They think it makes them weak and incapable. However, asking for help can be the most courageous thing, just for the simple fact that so many are afraid to ask. God didn't create everybody to know everything. In your areas of uncertainty or weakness, ask someone you trust for help. No matter how big or small your need may be, ask for help. There is nothing wrong with trying to accomplish a task by yourself, but if you start having trouble succeeding, and have done everything you know to do, ask a trusted peer for assistance. Maybe someone else has already gone through the same thing you are going through, perhaps they have already had experience with the very task you are trying to accomplish. There are many different people with many different areas of expertise in the world, so why try to do it all alone? You can be capable and still ask for help!

Reflection:

What is something in your life that you need help with right now?

____

____

____

Have you ever had to ask for help, even when you didn't want to? How did you feel in the end?

____

____

____

Challenge:

I challenge you to be brave and ask for help when you need it; don't try to do it all alone. I challenge you to offer support to others in need. I challenge you to pray to God daily for His grace and guidance in every situation of your life.

Words of Affirmation:

Yes, I need help, but I am still strong

I can ask for help yet be capable

Asking for help makes me brave

6

Beauty is All Around, Just Open Your Eyes!

Find Beauty in All Things

"The heavens declare the glory of God; the skies proclaim the work of His hands."

Psalm 19:1

Find beauty in all things

Through the good,

Through the bad,

Find beauty in all things

When your life is full of joy,

When you feel like you have hit rock bottom,

Find beauty in all things

It is so easy for us to go about our day without genuinely acknowledging the wondrous works of our Father. We so often take for granted the things and resources around us. Although it might not be our intention to take these things for granted, we walk through life without thanking God for the simple things; Grass for our cattle to eat, sunshine and rain for our crops to grow, the air around us allowing us to breathe, or even the ability of our senses. You must remember that no matter how bad your situation may be, there is always someone else who is worse off or less fortunate than you. Even on our worst days, we MUST find something that was good amid despair. If we begin only thinking of the bad, we will start to feel depression, hopelessness, defeat. However, if we can assess our day, and pick out at least one good thing, even if it's the fact that we are still alive, then we will open a window of hope and healing. Don't go throughout your day without pointing out some positives and thanking God for such things.

Reflection:

List at least one thing that was good about your day today.

____

____

____

Ask someone else what was good about their day and write it down here. It is good to encourage others to find the positive in their day as well.

____

____

____

Challenge:

I challenge you to keep a positive outlook on things, even when they aren't going the greatest. I challenge you to keep a notebook by your bed, and before you go to sleep at night, write down the good things that happen to you each day. I also challenge you to take time to thank God for the things you have written down.

Words of Affirmation:

Yes, not everything went great today, but (insert text) was my light in the darkness!

I am blessed

There is beauty in all things

7

There is a Light

Inside of You!

Let it Shine

Bright!

Let Your Light Shine Bright

"In the same way, let your light shine before others, that they may see your good deeds and glorify your Father in heaven."

Matthew 5:16

God placed a light inside of you, so let it shine

Show the world

Tell of His mighty works

God placed a light inside of you, so let it shine

Show compassion

Offer a helping hand

God placed a light inside of you, so let it shine

There is a light inside of you that strives to shine over any darkness. Do not ever be afraid to let your light shine bright. Let it shine so bright that it cannot be ignored. Let God's light shine inside of you, so that even those who do not know Him will come to know Him through you. How do you reach others with the light inside of you? Well, you must show compassion, love, patience, and much more. Try your very best to live as close to a Christlike life as possible. Strive to be happy, encouraging, and positive day end and day out. Smile and laugh because those things are contagious. Ask someone how their day was, write letters to those you love, compliment those you do not know. Be radiant and never let anything or anyone dim your light. Let it shine, and let it shine bright!

Reflection:

What do you think are some things that could dim your light?

___

___

___

What will you do in order to make sure your light stays shining bright, and how will you reach others with the light inside of you?

___

___

___

Challenge:

I challenge you to check in with yourself every day and make sure that you have not let anyone, or anything dim your light. I challenge you to pray each morning that the light God has placed inside of you will shine so bright that you can reach others and bring them closer to Christ.

Words of Affirmation:

My light shines bright in the darkness

God has placed a beautiful light inside of me, and I will let it shine bright

I will make a difference with the light that is inside of me

8

Because I Am a Child of God, I Am Forgiven!

Forgiven

"For no one is cast off by the Lord forever. Though He brings grief, He will show compassion, so great is His unfailing love."

Lamentations 3:31-32

You are forgiven

No mistake, big or small, can keep God from loving you

You are forgiven

We are human; we sin, but

We are forgiven

Repent to the Father

You are forgiven

No matter how big of a mistake you have made, you can always be forgiven. You might have consequences to deal with, but that does not mean God loves you any less. Nothing you can ever do will stop His love for you. If you ask for forgiveness, and genuinely mean it, then you can be forgiven. We all make mistakes, we all sin, so learn from your mistakes and move forward. Jesus died on the cross so that we can be forgiven of our sins and have another chance. Just as Christ forgives us, we must forgive ourselves and others. If Jesus, the most powerful being to ever walk this earth, died to forgive you of your sins, you should be able to find it in your heart to forgive others of the wrong that they have done to you. It might be hard, and it might take a little bit, but try your hardest to forgive. Forgiveness does not mean you have to be their best friend, but it does mean that you do not need to hold a grudge or resentment toward said person. So, forgive them and pray for them.

Reflection:

What does forgiveness look like to you?

____

____

____

How do you forgive someone who wrongs you? Have you ever had to forgive yourself for anything?

____

____

____

Challenge:

I challenge you to pray for those who have wronged or hurt you. I challenge you to forgive yourself for the things you think you cannot forgive yourself for. I challenge you to look back on your life and see if there is any residual resentment towards yourself or others. If there is, I challenge you to pray for that person and ask God to help you forgive and move on.

Words of Affirmation:

I am a child of God

I am forgiven

I will forgive

9

Stop Doubting. Your Blessing is Coming!

Stop Doubting

"Lord, when doubts fill my mind, when my heart is in turmoil, quiet me and me renewed hope and cheer."

Psalm 94:19

Stop doubting. Your blessing is coming

Continue walking the path God has set before you

Continue holding onto hope

Stop doubting. Your blessing is coming

Trust the process

Trust that God has your best interest at heart

Stop doubting. Your blessing is coming

God drops little blessings upon us every day. If you are reading this right now, God has blessed you with life. Blessings are all around, significant, small, evident, in disguise. You may be awaiting a specific blessing over yours or someone else's life right now. Well, hold onto the hope that God has heard your request, and is working on it right now. It might take much longer than you have anticipated; however, God's timing is the best. Stop with the doubting, and trust that God's logic is the best. He might not give you the blessing in the exact way that you wanted it, but He will continue to bless you day in and day out. Sometimes, He might not even give you the blessings that you thought were meant for you, but He sees our future and knows how it would play out if we were to receive certain things just the way we want. Therefore, His blessing might be not giving us exactly what we want.

Reflection:

What are a few of the biggest blessings that you have ever received?

____

____

____

Are you awaiting a huge blessing right now? What will you do when doubt creeps in? How will you respond if the blessing is not given to you in exactly the way you imagined?

____

____

____

Challenge:

I challenge you to pray God's will and not your own. I challenge you to keep an open and positive mind towards the blessings God will bestow upon you. I challenge you to take a look at your life and acknowledge all of the blessings that God has given you so far.

Words of Affirmation:

I am blessed

My blessings are coming; therefore, I will not doubt

God loves me and has my best interest at heart

10

Sometimes God Gives You Peace with Answers, but Most of the Time He Gives You the Peace without the Answers!

Peace without the Answers

"Peace I leave with you; my peace I give you. I do not give to you as the world gives. Do not let your hearts be troubled and do not be afraid."

John 14:27

Sometimes God gives us peace without the why

It might be hard to understand,

It might be hard to let go, but

Sometimes God gives us peace without the why

Do not go on a wild goose chase to find the answers,

Settle your worrying heart, because

Sometimes God gives us peace without the why

We all have questions about certain things that have happened in our lives. Questions like, "Why did this have to happen to me?" "How is this part of God's plan?" "What good could come from this?" These are tough questions that we have all thought about at one point or another. We pray and pray for God to reveal His plan, His reasoning behind such a big move. Well, sometimes He will give us those answers we were so desperately longing to hear. However, most times, He is just going to provide us with peace without knowing the why behind it all. That might not be what you want to hear, but we must learn to accept it, or we will run ourselves sick with worry. It's hard, and it might take a while to accept, but keep in mind that God works all things for the good of those who love Him. So, have peace in knowing that God has your best interest in mind, even if you do not understand it now.

Reflection:

Has there ever been a situation in your life where you have exhausted all possible answers?

____

____

____

Write down a time in your life where something happened completely out of your will but ended up working for your good.

____

____

____

Challenge:

I challenge you to pray for peace in every area of your life where you feel troubled. I challenge you to trust in God with everything you have. I challenge you to believe that whatever His reasoning is behind certain circumstances in your life, that they are all in your best interest.

Words of Affirmation:

God has my best interest in mind

I choose to live in peace

It is well with my soul

11

Have No Fear, Jesus is Always Here!

Fearless

"Even though I walk through the darkest valley, I will fear no evil, for You are with me; Your rod and your staff, they comfort me."

Psalm 23:4

Strive to be fearless

Do not let the world and its troubles bring you fear

Do not let the what-ifs and the what is to come bring you worry

Strive to be fearless

Trust that God is by your side

Trust that He will bring you through

Strive to be fearless

We serve a God who is so much more powerful than even your strongest fears. We tend to let fear creep in through the form of thoughts, images, words, etc. We hear about all the bad in the word, and rarely about the good. There is still good in the world. We cannot let fear dictate our future; we cannot let fear stop us from doing the things God has called us to do. There are going to be moments of uncertainty, but be confident that God is with you in those moments. There are going to be moments of pain and disappointment but know that God is near, and he is holding you close. When we set out to perform a task or reach a goal, we often let fear creep in. We fear failure and allow our thoughts, and the thoughts of the enemy, to set in and stop us short. Sometimes you might not make it on the first try, but you cannot let the fear of that be the reason you give up. Be brave, be fearless, take the leap. It will all be worth it in the end.

Reflection:

Has there ever been a time in your life where you let fear stop you from doing something important?

___

___

___

What will you choose to do next time fear creeps in and tries to lead you astray?

___

___

___

Challenge:

I challenge you to put faith over fear. I challenge you to pray and call upon the name of Jesus when doubt creeps in. I challenge you to leap when God tells you to, no matter how scary and unknown it might be.

Words of Affirmation:

I am fearless

I am courageous

I will no longer let fear control me

12

Why the Big Hurry? Slow Down, Catch Your Breath!

Slow Down

"Slow down. Take a deep breath. What's the big hurry? Why wear yourself out? Just what are you after, anyway?"

Jeremiah 2:25

Slow down, take your time

Why rush through life when you can enjoy it?

Slow down, take your time

Take it day by day

Take it step by step

Enjoy the life God has given you

Slow down, take your time

We are so quick to rush into things and to rush through things. Why are we always in such a big hurry? God has already mapped out your life; He has made a time and season for everything. Why rush? If it is meant for you, if you are meant to complete your task, then you will; God will see you through it. When we rush, we miss out on the little things, and we do not see the beauty through it all. Stop every now and then, and take a breath. Make sure that you are enjoying your task and are seeing it in all its incredible beauty. Mistakes start to form when we begin to rush. Do not just go through life like it is a race; instead, look at every step you take as if you are taking the scenic route. Enjoy life, do not hurry it along.

Reflection:

Have you ever rushed into a decision and later realized that maybe you should have taken your time and thought more about it? Have you ever rushed through a season of your life and later realized that you should have slowed down and paid closer attention to all the beautiful little details around you?

Where is an area of your life that you want to slow down and take in every beautiful moment?

____

____

____

Challenge:

I challenge you to slow time, take your time. I challenge you to choose the scenic route through life. Do not merely exist; you must live. If it is meant for you, it will still be there when you get around to it. I challenge you to pray about every single decision you come across and be patient in receiving an answer. I challenge you to pay attention to the beauty around you.

Words of Affirmation:

I choose to enjoy the little things in life

I will not rush my way through life, but will instead take it step by step

If it is meant for me, it will wait for me; God's timing is best

13

We are all human, we all feel, and that is okay!

Feelings

"A time to weep, a time to laugh; a time to mourn, and a time to dance."

Ecclesiastes 3:4

It is okay to have feelings and to let them show,

Sadness and Joy

Grief and Celebration

It is okay to have feelings and to let them show

Feelings are a part of life

Feelings are what make us human

It is okay to have feelings and to let them show

Some moments in life are filled with pure joy, some moments are filled with heartache, and other moments we might not know what exactly we are feeling or why. It is okay to have those feelings and to let them play out; just do not let your feelings and emotions stand in your way of doing the things that you are called to do. Do not let your feelings overtake your entire life. We often try to suppress all emotion that is not joy. We let it all bottle up, and then it eventually explodes. Instead, how about we try talking to a trusted peer. When you are feeling overwhelmed with emotions, talk them out. If you are not comfortable sharing your feelings, talk to God, He is always there to listen. Ask God for clarity as to what you are feeling or why you are feeling it. Ask God for peace and comfort. It is okay to cry when you are upset. It is okay to laugh when you feel joy. Do not feel bad about having feelings.

Reflection:

What emotions are you feeling in this moment?

____

____

____

If the above emotions are along the lines of sadness or stress, how will you go about turning those into happy ones? If they are happy emotions, what will you do to continue having those joyful emotions?

____

____

____

Challenge:

I challenge you to allow yourself to feel, allow yourself to go through the different stages of emotions. However, I challenge you to make sure you do not let your emotions get the best of you. I challenge you to acknowledge your feelings while also talking them out with a trusted peer or God.

Words of Affirmation:

It is okay for me to feel

I will seek out the joy in even the worst situations

God cares about me and my emotions

14

Be like a child and have that stubbornness that you can do anything!

Childlike Faith

"So, the Lord blessed Job in the second half of his life even more than in the beginning."

Job 42:12

Have childlike faith

Through the waiting and the wondering

Have childlike faith

Through the struggle and the victory

Have childlike faith

Just because we have a terrible chapter, does not mean our story has to have a terrible ending. Be like a child and have that stubbornness that you can do anything! Believe with all your heart that if God is in it, nothing is impossible. We talk about having faith during the hard times and challenges, which is extremely important, but we must also have faith in the victory. We must believe that God will continue to work through that win. We cannot go through life, wondering if our success will be short-lived. We are to have confidence and determination in believing that God will carry out our victory. We must understand that whatever comes next, God already has a solution long before the problem ever even arises! When you give something over to God, you must give it entirely. Do not say you surrender it to God yet still hover over it to make sure God is handling it okay. He is the all-mighty, all-powerful God, and He can handle it himself. So, I say to you, have childlike faith through every single circumstance of life! Do not stress about what comes next!

Reflection:

Has there been an instance in your life where if you had practiced childlike faith, your worry and stress would have been so much less?

____

____

____

Where is a current area of your life that you need to practice childlike faith?

____

____

____

Challenge:

I challenge you to practice childlike! I challenge you to have that childlike mentality that you can do anything! I challenge you to keep God the center of everything and put 100% faith and confidence in Him.

Words of Affirmation:

I will make it through this

Everything is going to be okay because God's hand is in it

15

Loving Everyone does not mean You Have to be their Best Friend!

Love Everyone

"Love thy neighbor as yourself."

Matthew 22:39

Love everyone

We are called by God to love everyone

We are called by God to lead others to Christ

Love everyone

You do not have to follow in their footsteps

You do not have to be their best friend but,

Love everyone

God calls us to love our neighbors. Loving your neighbor does not mean you have to be their best friend or even have a relationship with them. However, as Christ-followers, we must show the love that Christ has shown us. We have sinned time and time again. We have committed wrongful actions at one time or another; however, God forgave us repeatedly. He forgives us repeatedly. He loves us no matter the path we have traveled. He tells us to love even our enemies, and after everything He has done for us, we owe it to him to grant that wish. Love also the ones that have wronged you. Love even the ones you find it nearly impossible to love. Loving someone does not mean you have to agree with what they do, nor does it mean you have to create a relationship with them, love them as Christ loves you. Pray for them daily, pray that God will reach their heart. Pray that whatever their wrongdoings are will be forgiven and that they will find Christ. I understand this is easier said than done, and even I struggle with this one, but I will try my very best to love my neighbors because that is what God is asking of me.

Reflection:

Is there someone in your life that you need to work on loving?

____

____

____

What will you do the next time you come across someone who wrongs you?

____

____

____

Challenge:

I challenge you to add those who have wronged you to your prayer list. I challenge you to work hard to love everyone, even if that does not mean forming a relationship with them. I challenge you to remember that Christ loves us even if He does not agree with our actions; therefore, we should do the same with our peers.

Words of Affirmation:

I am loved

I will show love

I will strive to pray for those who have wronged me

16

No Matter How Lonely You Feel, you are Never Alone!

You are Never Alone

"Whether you turn to the right or the left, your ears will hear a voice behind you saying, 'This is the way; walk in it.'"

Isaiah 30:21

You are never alone

A journey into the great unknown

A time of trouble

You are never alone

A triumphant celebration

A time of pure joy

You are never alone

Although we cannot physically see God, He is ALWAYS there! He will never leave you, nor will He forsake you. Even when it feels like you are all alone, remember that God is all around, He is holding your hand and guiding you. If you are keeping God the center of your life, He will see you through all of the plans He has for your life. Even if you do not have anyone in your life that you can 100% trust, have comfort in knowing that you can 100% trust in God. People are not entirely reliable, they might not always be there when you need them, but God is always there. Just because you do not see a physical being, have peace in believing that you have the most powerful being ever to exist standing by your side fighting your battles for you. If you fall, He is there to pick you up. If you need a shoulder to cry on, God is right there, holding you close. You are never alone.

Reflection:

Has there ever been a time in your life where you have felt completely alone?

____

____

____

How does it make you feel to know that God is by your side every single moment of your life?

____

____

____

Challenge:

I challenge you to thank God daily for never leaving you. I challenge you to remember that He is a trusted friend and Father that you can talk to about anything. I challenge you to remember that there is someone that has your back constantly.

Words of Affirmation:

I am never alone

I always have someone watching my back

Jesus loves me and protects me

17

Action Speak Louder than Words, but Kind Words are Helpful Too!

Actions and Words

"So whatever you wish that others would do to you, also do to them, for this is the Law and the Prophets."

Matthew 7:12

Actions speak louder than words, but kind words are helpful too

Live your life as Christ would want you to

Before you act, before you speak, ask yourself if Jesus would approve

Actions speak louder than words, but kind words are helpful too

Hold a door open for a stranger

Compliment someone in some way

Actions speak louder than words, but kind words are helpful too

We have all heard of the "sticks and stones" saying. The truth is, words do hurt. We can choose to let certain things in, but even if we decide not to believe said things, it still stings. While I believe that actions do speak louder than words, I also believe that we need to choose kind words as well. Be the kind of disciples God calls us to be. The kind of disciples that go above and beyond. Hold a door open for someone and compliment them on their way in. Not only will it make them feel good, but it will also help you feel good as well. Do kind deeds, but also use kind words. Strive to put a smile on at least one person's face a day. Strive to do acts of kindness while training your tongue to speak life and joy into someone's existence. Strive to be the best version of you that you can be by practicing both positive actions and words. They do go hand in hand.

Reflection:

What are some nice actions and words that someone has blessed you with? How did they make you feel?

____

____

____

List at least 3 acts of kindness and 3 compliments that you will someone this week.

____

____

____

Challenge:

I challenge you to do random acts of kindness throughout your day. I challenge you to make someone smile. I challenge you to write a letter to three people, it does not have to be long, and practice using kind words; tell them how much they mean to you, compliment their personality, make them feel good about themselves.

Words of Affirmation:

I will strive to do and say kind things

I can be the reason someone smiles today

God blesses me; therefore, I will bless others

18

Change is Bound to Happen, so why Fight it?

Change

"I, the Lord, do not change. Therefore you, the descendants of Jacob, are not destroyed."

Malachi 3:6

Change is inevitable

Big or small

Exciting or scary

Change is inevitable

Do your best to adapt to it

Always trust God through it

Change is inevitable

Change is going to occur several times throughout our life. Change can be hard, but it is not always a bad thing. Maybe God is bringing about change in your life so that He can clear a path for a big blessing that He is about to reveal. Perhaps He is bringing change so that we can get back on the road we have strayed from. Whatever the change is that is going on in your life, just know that there is a bigger picture. I think the reason that change is so difficult is because we get used to the way things are going. Therefore, when something new and different comes along, we tend to shy away because it is an unknown. However, what if we instead accept the change and thank God for what He is about to do. Do not miss out on opportunities because you are afraid. Remember this: God's Love for you never changes. It forever remains the same, and that love is far beyond compare.

Reflection:

What has been a huge change in your life? How did you feel about that change?

____

____

____

How will you react next time you are going through a change?

____

____

____

Challenge:

I challenge you to be more open to change. I challenge you to pray through it and thank God for the things He is about to do in your life. I challenge you to look on the bright side of things and pick out a few positives about the change you are going through.

Words of Affirmation:

Change can be good

I can adapt to change

God's Love is one thing that will never change

19

Maybe the things you had in mind are not the same as what God has in mind. He knows best!

Disappointments

"Many are the plans in a man's heart, but it is the Lord's purpose that will stand."

Proverbs 19:21

Not everything goes according to our plan

Not everything happens just when we think it will

God's plan is sometimes different than yours

When your plans go haywire

When your dreams seem to be put on hold, do not give up

God's plan is sometimes different than yours

Maybe the very things that you thought were meant for you weren't what God had in mind. Perhaps the dreams you have been dreaming seem to be put on hold. Maybe the things that you have been working towards do not have the results you had hoped they would. Do not give up hope; do not let them keep you from striving for other things. Sometimes God redirects our path for reasons that are unknown to us but known to Him. We must trust that God knows what is coming next and that He has our best interest at heart. Maybe He is keeping you from imminent danger; perhaps He has something even bigger and better in mind for us. I know that it can be disappointing when things do not go your way, but just let every disappointment be a call to worship. Thank God for the work He is doing in you. Thank God for the blessings He has coming your way. Most of all, thank God for knowing your heart and just what you need when you need it.

Reflection:

What is something in your life that did not turn out the way you thought? How did you cope with it? How will you cope the next time?

___

___

___

Did you end up having a bigger and better result later down the road?

___

___

___

Challenge:

I challenge you to be patient when things do not go your way; maybe it is for the greater good. I challenge you to thank God daily for the redirections He has given you. I challenge you to pray for God's will to be done above all else.

Words of Affirmation:

I will trust God

I will praise God even during disappointment

God knows just what I need and when I need it

20

Family is Who You Make of it!

Family is More than Just Blood

"We love because He first loved us."

1 John 4:19

Family is more than just blood

Someone who brightens your day

Someone who keeps you going in the right direction

Family is more than just blood

Someone you can talk to about anything

Someone whose opinion you truly value

Family is more than just blood

Family is what you make of it. Just because you do not share blood does not mean that you cannot be family. God places people in your life who lift you up and keep you accountable. Some people God has placed in my life are more family to me than even some of my blood relatives. They make me laugh, and they are always there to talk and give advice. They are great examples of what a Christlike life should look portray. They are the type of people who I know I can call at two o'clock in the morning if I need someone to talk to. They are the people who will not judge me, the type of people who will tell me if I need to make a change in my life to better it, the type of people who can give me a good laugh at just the right times. You see, family is what you make of it. Family is more than only blood. They are the ones you trust wholeheartedly. They are a breath of fresh air. Find yourself some good family!

Reflection:

Do you have people in your life who you are not related to, but you call them family?

____

____

____

Are these people positive influences/role models in your life?

____

____

____

Challenge:

I challenge you to grow your family, find people who lift you up and encourage you daily. I challenge you to improve your relationship with those whom God has placed in your life. I challenge you to surround yourselves with positive peers and to also spread some positivity to those around you as well.

Words of Affirmation:

I am loved by many

My family is who I make of it

God loves me and wants me to be surrounded by others who love me

ABOUT THE AUTHOR

Cheyenne Moody is a God-fearing, God-loving woman. She loves to encourage others and see them unlock their full potential. When not spending time with family and friends, Cheyenne loves going to the barn and spending quality time with her horse. She loves to be outdoors, surrounded by all of God's beautiful creations. For a free, more in-depth, and extended version of each devotional, visit her blog page at www.simplylavished.com

I hope that you enjoyed my devotional! I pray that it gives you inspiration, peace, joy, and insight. I pray many blessings upon you and yours.

–Cheyenne

*Always remember that you are lavished in God's Love, it's that simple! *

Made in the USA
Monee, IL
24 December 2019